Daughter of God

Para Mary:

Con cariño y respeto.

Carmen y Capi

Daughter of God

Verlaine Crawford

High Castle Publishing

Another Book By Verlaine Crawford: *Ending the Battle Within, How to Create a Harmonious Life Working with Your Sub-Personalities.* Audio tapes by Verlaine are also available.

For information address:

High Castle Publishing
25108-B Marguerite Parkway, Suite 511
Mission Viejo, CA 92692
Phone: 500-442-Angel (2643)
Fax: 500-442-Love (5683)
web site: www.daughterofgod.com

FIRST EDITION: August 1998

Distributed in the United States by BookWorld Companies

Painting on front cover by Lena Liu.
Prints of Guardian Angel, Angel of Love and Angel of Light
and other works of art by Lena Liu are available through
High Castle Publishing at 500-442-Angel (2643).

Cover Design by Lightbourne Images, Ashland, OR

Printed by Bang Printing, Brainerd, MN

Library of Congress Cataloging in Publication Data

Crawford, Verlaine, 1943-
        Daughter of God: Angelic Messages of Wisdom and Love
        1. Inspirational 2. Angels 3. Spiritual 4. New Age I. Title.

Contents

Contents

This book is dedicated
to all who believe in angels
and to the grand angels of light
who are guiding the people on earth.

The Meeting

*"And the angel said unto them, Fear not:
for, behold, I bring you good tidings of great joy,
which shall be to all people."* Luke 2:10

The tall, majestic pines swayed in the swirling gusts of wind as the mountain path opened into a gallery of sculptured rock formations. The timeless quality of nature echoed through giant primordial boulders which stood proudly as a grand tribute to the Master Sculptor.

I struggled to catch my breath, climbing alone toward the summit outlined by an azure sky. Whispers of clouds were forming, expanding, billowing up and then crashing like silent waves over the ancient pinnacles of earth's thrust toward the heavens.

I caught a glimpse far below of the distant valley, hidden in a soft mist which veiled the once familiar roads and

The Meeting

market places. I had also lived among the masses of humanity now covering the fertile soil which in the past supported orchards and farmlands stretching from the mountains westward to the sea. The vision was only a faint memory of what seemed like another lifetime.

The air became thinner and my breathing deepened as the winding trail rose higher. I could see that only the most courageous pine trees managed to hold root and bravely push their twisted branches skyward.

Feeling lightheaded, I sat on a chiseled rock observing the gigantic boulders around me and thought, What secrets do you hold? Have you kept watch through the centuries? If you could speak, what stories would you tell?

The silence was broken by the sound of wings circling overhead. A magnificent hawk soared above the ridge, spiraling, lifting, weaving dream circles in the rising air. My mind drifted away, and for a moment it felt as though I were floating within the hawk and looking through his eyes at the trees and rocks below.

My attention was quickly brought back to my body as a gust of wind rippled over my clothes. The solitary cry of the hawk pierced my heart, and I was flooded with emotions from the past. Tears streamed down my face as memories filled with pain and sorrow overwhelmed me.

The Meeting

The warmth of the sun slowly dried my tears as I gathered my composure and summoned the strength to continue my arduous pilgrimage. Ascending much higher along the serpentine pathway, I had nearly reached the base of the final ascent to the peak when the steepness eased and I could breathe easier.

The path then narrowed, and I felt powerful waves of energy passing through me as I entered a hallway lined by immense boulders. Each of the imposing pillars of granite appeared to be placed strategically, forming a corridor that was alive with mysterious forces emanating from these awesome guardians of the mountain heights.

Shivers ran up my spine. A memory flashed before me of a similar experience in Egypt where I had walked beneath the massive carved columns which adorned the entrance to the mystical temple of Karnak.

Moving through the long, winding corridor, a sense of eeriness crept over me. I had a strange feeling that I was being watched. Out of the corner of my eye, I saw specters of mystifying images rising to the surface of the huge stones. The shivers along my back became even more electric, and I started walking faster.

Around the next bend, I was suddenly aware of my destination: *The Window.*

The Meeting

There in front of me was an open portal framed by immense, angled formations of stone. Rough hewn monoliths had fallen together perfectly to create a large square window in the wall of rocks.

I crawled up an incline and into the opening where I stood entranced by the spectacular sight before me. The sheer face of the mountain presented a facade of enormous, white palisades crowned with gleaming granite spires.

Climbing through the passageway, I emerged into a protected area out of the wind. In the hushed calmness, the veil of time and space seemed to lift around me.

I moved over broken boulders and out onto a narrow precipice overlooking a forest below. Pausing for a moment, I absorbed the view which had widened to reveal a beautiful, hidden valley surrounded by towering cliffs. Looking more closely, I could see glistening ponds nestled among the trees and rolling green meadows.

Hugging the sheer wall of stone, I edged my way carefully along a narrow lip of granite until I could pull myself up onto a recessed shelf which had been carved and smoothed by the elements. Resting upon this lordly throne, I leaned back into the cool shelter formed by the rock's curved embrace. A feeling of quietness enveloped me. I took a deep breath, closed my eyes and began to drift away.

The Meeting

My dizziness faded into deep contentment, and time passed without my awareness. I floated in a state of tranquility until I felt a warm, tingling sensation move over my face, as if the sun were shining on me, though I was sitting in full shade. A moment later, I was awash in brilliant light.

When I opened my eyes, the light became even brighter. Gradually, the shimmering opalescence took the form of a beautiful angel hovering in the air before me. Dressed in a flowing, gossamer gown, she appeared motionless as her translucent wings became visible. Behind her the rocks were transforming into finely sculpted columns connected by a sweeping arch.

The angelic presence became ever more defined. She smiled with knowing eyes which seemed to look deep into my soul. Her glowing halo expanded and surrounded me in an aura of Divine Love.

Questions were tumbling through my mind as I heard her melodious voice say, "Be at peace."

Speechless, I thought, Why are you here?

She answered, "You have prayed many times to know God's will for your life."

"Yes," I replied, trembling. "I have."

The angel floated closer. "This meeting was planned long ago. The time has come again for spiritual wisdom to

The Meeting

shine upon mankind and awaken their souls. The illusion cast by darkness will be seen as a mere lack of light."

I wondered to myself, Who is she? Why has she come?

"I am a messenger of God's Love, an ancient immortal, one of the legions of angelic hosts. We are the translators of Universal Wisdom into words you will understand. It is our calling to rekindle your awareness that you are spiritual beings who have entered physical form to live and create as sons and daughters of God.

"Few humans remember their true heritage. You are everlasting souls who have come to grow from your many experiences. You are reflections of the image of God taking part in the unfoldment of life's grand design. Every person has a unique contribution to give toward the creation of heaven on earth."

"What can I do?" I asked.

"You will be given teachings to share which have the power to transform the hearts and minds of those longing to walk the golden path of love and wisdom."

"Why me?" I asked.

"You were chosen because of your desire to share love and compassion and your willingness to follow Divine Guidance. Be aware that we place not a burden upon you,

but present gifts to be given to the many people who are ready to receive.

"Have faith, and let this be your joy, for we are watching over you, hearing your every prayer and aware of all your needs. When you open your heart and mind, we will fill you with visions and words of inspiration which you will transcribe and share with others."

She looked into my eyes, and I felt a slight pressure on my temples. Within seconds, I was out of my body and suspended, floating like a feather next to this lovely being. As I looked around, all of nature was glowing with light.

Then my gaze was drawn down the cliff to menacing rocks far below. Fear and doubt gripped me. I lost my sense of equilibrium and began spinning out of control. I was falling into the valley when the angel touched my arm and steadied me. Her warmth dissolved my fears, and I relaxed into the feeling of weightless flight.

Moments later I was back in my physical form on the ledge, staring at the angel who was now fading from view. I heard her say, "We will meet again soon."

An afterglow permeated my being with a sense that I had been touched by the Eternal. Patterns of creation glimmered like a dewy mist before my eyes. I drifted in an atmosphere of love, entranced by the glory of the Divine.

The Meeting

The first hues of violet and rose shimmered across the sky announcing the beginning of sunset. I climbed back through the window and turned to look at the magical portal which had led me to glimpse another world.

Moving along the hallway of boulders, I bid farewell to the sleeping giants who had greeted me. Walking briskly, barely touching the ground, I hurried down the winding mountain path through the shadowy forms of spreading oaks and tall pines.

In the waning light, I reached the trailhead and followed a dirt road which led to the outskirts of town. Finally, I approached my home where the last rays of sun were highlighting the two stone pillars which flanked the entrance to the driveway. Each was topped by a golden sentinel, an eagle and a lion, welcoming my return.

Against the stillness of evening, a gentle wind rustled through the trees. I strolled out onto an open area of rounded granite overlooking the forest which was framed by the amber silhouette of the mountains.

The majesty of Tahquitz Peak balanced the regal splendor of Lily Rock, painted a soft rose in the sunset. Sitting silently, I relived my wondrous visitation on the summit. The light dimmed, and I entered my rustic retreat as the first stars began to shine in the dark blue sky.

The Meeting

In the twilight of evening, I sat sipping warm tea near the huge rock fireplace. A sparkling fire sent patterns of light dancing around the room. Through the window I could see a full moon rising over the ridge where the pathway had led me to the edge of eternity.

The atmosphere was fluid with warmth as a night wind blew against the window panes. I was immersed in feelings of gratitude and love. A faint glow became visible above me as my pen touched the paper. Images and words began flowing like celestial music through my mind.

An angelic voice said, "Let us begin the teachings with Love..."

Love

L ove is the power of the seen and unseen,
    underlying the grandeur of the universe
    in countless galaxies, spinning, whirling,
    held within the Creator's warm embrace.
    Love emerges as a boundless, rising tide
    sweeping compassion and understanding
    over the fortress walls of fear and confusion.
Flooding the lowlands of sadness and regret,
    love lifts and sustains you effortlessly
    above the mountain heights of ecstasy.

Lovers of life celebrate nature's wonder
    through the artistry of fine textures and colors
    found in glimmering sunlight on autumn leaves
    and towering peaks crested in winter snow,
    fields of flowers dancing in the spring breeze,
    desert lightning awakened by summer heat,
    and starlit skies as timeless guardians of night.
Brilliant hues glisten upon tranquil seas
    with cloudscape silhouettes shaping the horizon,
    warmly wrapping you in creation's mystery.

Love holds, releases, fills, empties, fills again,
    expanding into forever your heart's desires.
    Symphonic harmonies float on the balmy eve
    as ocean waves caress the sandy shore.
    Moments of rapture, a warm touch, a sweet kiss,
    two souls intertwined in heavenly bliss,
    drawn into enchantment as time slips away.
Looking deep within, you find a vast expanse,
    celestial spheres grander than the heavens above,
    beyond space and time, a realm of peace to share.

Love weaves golden threads into patterns of life,
    a rich tapestry bejeweled with memories,
    timeless treasures, remembrances of moments
    when love bestowed gifts of peace sublime.
    Love is given and received in every breath,
    for love is the very essence of who you are,
    echoing promises of where your journey leads.
You are love's gracious host and honored guest.
    Love has created you, love is your pathway,
    love guides you, and love is your destiny.

Identity

When asked who you are, do you pause and ponder,
  or respond with a name that was given at birth?
  Is your banner knowledge or power bestowed?
  Do you stand as beliefs and values maintained
  or see yourself only as talents and skills,
  accomplishments past or those still to come,
  or are you the feelings you express or withhold?
Could you be the persona seen by the world,
  portraying your role through laughter or tears,
  acting in daydreams disclosed or concealed?

You are not your profession or work that you do,
  not merely your thoughts or actions performed,
  for you exceed your awards, stature and standing.
  Greater than emotions spilling forth from your heart,
  surpassing schooling and all you have learned,
  you are above possessions you have or have not
  and are even much grander than all of your dreams.
As a spiritual being living on earth,
  you reveal the intention behind all creation,
  by your light you witness the darkness dispelled.

Identity

Surrendering concepts you once held as true,
      assuming the view of a distant observer,
      you are no longer tied to the ways of the world.
      Catching the wind, you will glide far above,
      reaching the freedom for which you have longed.
      And alighting upon the highest of mountains,
      you will bathe in glory and draw close to the throne.
Transcending beyond the earthly dimensions,
      you will behold a magnificent vision
      and know the truth of your own perfection.

In your radiance, you appear as angels,
      sparkling like gold in the glistening sunlight.
      You have dreams undreamt and songs to be sung
      with abilities untapped for you to be shown.
      You are love beyond measure to feel and to share,
      a light shining forth with unlimited brilliance
      and a source of wisdom that flows from within.
As the sons and daughters of the One Most High,
      you are made in the image of Spirit Divine,
      forever reflecting the resplendence of God.

Purpose

M otionless among the trees, the grand elk stands,
hiding behind branches, nearly invisible.
Keenly aware while watching and waiting,
the elk knows the moment to answer the call
and break his stance to bound over the knoll.
Your fear and uncertainty may find you frozen
with a need for direction to make your next move.
Can you remember when you heard a calling
which stirred your heart to beat with new meaning,
surging with excitement welling up from within?

The purpose you sensed is echoing inside,
with a network of choices leading you onward,
presenting a vista that sweeps out before you
where dreams may be followed and miracles sown.
Watching for sign posts to stay on the high road,
heeding the cry of fellow travelers in need,
you may offer a hand for their steps to be eased.
In the search for your mission, truth will unfold
with guidance given to enlighten your soul
and transform the mundane into great splendor.

Purpose

With selfless intent your strength becomes boundless;
 the forces of nature can be beckoned or stilled
 when you serve as an instrument of Divine Will.
 The quest for answers to all of your questions
 is put to rest with the doubts you have known,
 and desires for riches and personal glory
 are replaced by the wealth your spirit may show.
Witnessing works of miraculous nature,
 abounding with peace that enriches your soul,
 you release constraints to be humble yet bold.

There is no person identical to you,
 unique in creation to add your vision
 and play your own part in the overall plan.
 Do not misjudge the importance of actions;
 like ripples on water, they expand through the world,
 and unknown to you are your blessings in motion
 with each act of kindness touching people untold.
If you yearn for purpose to inspire your days,
 be steadfast and strive for the highest of goals,
 find heaven within and return filled with love.

Intuition

Intuition floats on the hem of the maiden
     and tugs at the cuff of the tender youth.
     Your inner knowing enhances discernment,
     watching, waiting, and always preparing
     to assist you with subtle, yet sure direction.
     Heightening senses and inspiring your thoughts,
     it will help you to find your higher life purpose.
Like a candle glowing in darkness of night,
     your insight illumines the realms unknown,
     presenting keys to unlock the great mysteries.

Eternal guidance is flowing within you,
     always closer than your very next breath,
     awaiting your consent and silent request.
     Emerging amidst confusion and turmoil,
     whispers of counsel can be heard in your heart,
     calming your mind and soothing your spirit,
     revealing both perils and pathways to take.
Though emotions may cloud your clear perception
     and lead you astray to be lost for awhile,
     intuition abides as your fountain of truth.

Intuition

A gentle reminder of that which you know,
  your vision awakens from sleepless slumber,
  shedding veils of deceit like scales from your eyes,
  with the glass wiped clean to see through illusions.
  The route ahead is lined with great challenge,
  beckoning you onward and testing resolve,
  disclosing the ways you may savor each moment.
Insight reads clues from an invisible map,
  showing the turns on your maze-like path
  which lead to scenes of fulfillment and promise.

A labyrinth of choices spreads before you
  as you learn what to welcome and when to pass by,
  which people to trust and the timing for action.
  Aware of motives and secret intentions,
  you hear the meaning between words spoken,
  perceive through masks of image and pretense,
  and sense what is hidden beyond explanation.
Trusting intuition your sight is renewed
  as angels enfold you in wings of their love,
  lifting your spirit to view your true destiny.

Friendship

Friendship billows bright like a schooner's full sails
  carrying you high and fast on the wind.
  A trusted shipmate signs on for the tour
  to help chart a passage through oceans of time.
  Listening, yearning, and learning together,
  waiting with patience through stillness and calm,
  you are ready to weather the fiercest of storms.
With unspoken pacts, you give understanding,
  lending a hand and laughing through tears,
  two seafarers casting for fortunes and pleasures.

Sitting on deck, watching the waves rolling by,
  words float softly on a cool summer's breeze.
  Sharing the stories of youth's innocent folly,
  unearthing treasures of memories long buried,
  revealing secrets that had long been concealed,
  releasing emotions clutched tightly for years,
  you receive acceptance, and trust is upheld.
A sense of agreement strengthens your purpose
  as allies catch thoughts like precious raindrops
  and drink from one cup to quench the same thirst.

Friendship

Comraderie stands as tall masts of a ship
      set deep in the hull to reach lofty heights,
      and climbing among the great spreading yardarms,
      you search the horizon on rigging stretched tight.
      The quarters below offer rest from the cold
      as a sheltered retreat where wounds may be healed;
      with care and assurance your sorrows are soothed.
You duel with sharp words, yet no blood is drawn,
      sailing together through life's open waters
      with a partner who honors your humor and style.

Working and playing without effort or qualm,
      enhancing the ties of a deepening kinship,
      protecting, defending and bringing a smile,
      your souls are enriched by adventures you share.
      When sailing beneath the dark skies of winter,
      your fellowship warms and brightens the days
      to steady your bearings and hold your true course.
Keeping each promise with faithful devotion,
      dismissing the losses, rejoicing in triumph,
      your friendship allows you to rise once again.

Male & Female

From the field of light your consciousness is born,
an eternal impression of the cosmic form
which descends to earth as a woman or man.
Duality is nature's response to life's plan,
breeding a powerful magnet of opposites
which binds and directs your compelling desire
to find a companion with whom you feel whole.
Intense attraction and unexplained passion
express the mysterious essence of gender
as the dawning of need to reach the Divine.

Society attempts to define each child,
shaping emotions and prescribing intentions,
stating the conduct and demeanor required.
Told to be passive, girls shroud their ambition,
and boys are encouraged to hide soft affection.
A quandary arises without your awareness
when you have denied a part of your soul.
The balance point between feelings and actions
is a sacred site that dwells deep within
where conflict ends and peace can endure.

Male & Female

Contrasting forces are woven within you;
>the male dynamic focuses outward
>while the female aspect spirals inward.
>When balanced the masculine gives and creates,
>but if uncontrolled, it may force and destroy.
>In balance the feminine receives and embraces,
>but when unrestrained it may grasp and ensnare.
The seeds of creation bloom through the female,
>and the male is inspired to create with action
>as the spirit and soul form their union in all.

At your core you may sense a wellspring calling
>to find the source of the feminine mystery,
>rooted in the earth and welcoming heaven.
>Like gossamer lingering on a silent wind,
>the spirit, son of God, is your life force moving.
>Daughter of God, your soul, absorbs experience
>and speaks in the language of poetry.
The center of being is undivided,
>a meeting place where polarities merge,
>the manifest and mystical blending as one.

Marriage

From yearning borne in the depths of your being,
    you have chosen to join your hopes and dreams
    and to walk side by side on your special journey.
    Uniting your lives to discover life's treasures,
    your hearts will unfold in the meaning of love:
    to know and be known, to give and receive,
    to inspire and be lifted in grateful devotion.
You will rest in lush valleys and scale grand heights,
    as lovers and friends you will soar through the sky
    to magnificent realms where your spirits may dwell.

Feeling a longing reaching through the ages,
    you were drawn together to merge in affection,
    interweaving the caring that both of you bring
    to help one another in times of your need.
    Ascending the branches of the Tree of Life,
    each step affirms your promise is honored
    to form the foundation from which you will grow.
Beholding the vision of your beloved,
    you are carried along in a state of bliss,
    revealing the magic of romantic design.

Marriage

Love is a mirror of polished reflection
     with the image of beauty perceived from within,
     displaying the essence of all your desires.
     Sharing the quest of expanding awareness
     with courage to face an uncertain future,
     in holy union you will rise above challenge
     as a living testament to the power of love.
Expressing your feelings and living your truth,
     you open your spirit and unveil your soul;
     as travelers in faith, two flames become one.

Know that angels are bestowing their blessings
     through celestial choirs blending in harmony,
     singing of gifts far more precious than gold,
     which you will receive in moments of silence.
     Enjoined by your vows of loving surrender,
     a glowing aura of wonder surrounds you
     which glorifies the Maker of all that is known.
Marriage celebrates love's deepest communion,
     a radiant expression of hearts intertwined
     as you share the sweet taste of eternal wine.

Children

A ngelic faces stare at you with wonder,
    asking to be gathered into your arms.
    So innocent and open, in need of your caring,
    children offer the smiles of a love that is pure.
    Intimate kinship becomes deeply rooted,
    increasing the bonds with each passing day
    as both parent and child are in soul united.
Through unwavering love, their sense of self grows,
    and with little to fear, they enter life's stage
    as natural actors to perform in the world.

With great expectations their stories unfold,
    catching hints of tomorrow in all they perceive.
    Molding creation with tiny strong hands,
    their visions take form like castles of sand.
    Assurance and patience will give them courage
    to raise up their voices and offer their songs
    and sing from the heart of dreams to be shared.
Imagination when free looks far and wide
    for a cast of friends to take part in the play
    while hiding and seeking to find who they are.

Children

Light is reflected as the sun upon moon,
    a mirror to see what impression is shown.
    Following clues as if searching for treasure,
    children observe the events all around them,
    copying or rejecting others' actions and deeds,
    measuring rewards while weighing their choices,
    and with endless questions, they search for the truth.
Every small detail is closely observed,
    they learn by example, not proclamation,
    responding to feelings behind all the words.

To mature as they must, young wings will be spread
    to fly toward a future unknown and uncharted,
    longing to embrace the fulfillment of wishes,
    held aloft by excitement to follow their dreams.
    Building on the strength of long held traditions,
    each new generation moves forward with pride
    to blaze fresh trails and discover true fortune.
Born with their talents and purpose of spirit,
    children will thrive when encouraged to grow
    and will blossom in beauty when tended with love.

Health

The jaguar climbs steadily over the rocks,
　　　catching the first rays of dawn through the trees.
　　　The night was for feasting; she now settles in
　　　with cubs by her side to nap through the day.
　　　Some time for rest and the chase will begin;
　　　with swiftness and endurance as vital friends,
　　　she will go on the hunt for food in the wild.
Mankind once lived in harmony with nature;
　　　strategy and patience expanded the mind,
　　　and the needs of survival strengthened the form.

Children delight in the feeling of motion,
　　　moving with ease and a sense of freedom,
　　　curling their bodies into tight round balls,
　　　turning cartwheels and summersaults over the grass,
　　　flowing and fluid with no thoughts of fear,
　　　darting to and fro like new born fawns,
　　　prancing and playing for the joy of sensation.
Remain in your youth and forget to grow old,
　　　for there are no rules that you must slow down;
　　　the world can be seen from a young point of view.

Health

Your life has seasons profound in their changes,
      and when winds of danger howl at your door,
      you begin to respond with natural defenses,
      preparing for retreat or standing your ground.
      Each of your cells is aroused for engagement;
      primordial instincts may rise up and control,
      yet seldom are threats well-founded or clear.
The urgent peril for you in this moment
      is holding the posture of tension and fear,
      for illness emerges when you have grown weary.

Release your tears to fall softly behind you,
      and leave cares in the past along with your pain.
      Offer toasts to health as a wish to be given,
      though it must be claimed by actions you choose.
      You can work in a garden with sweat on your brow,
      climb on a path until your breathing is full,
      stretch with the sunrise or dance through the night.
When your goal is greater than living more years,
      you will strive for a vision of true well being;
      add peace and compassion—be lighthearted!

Home

Throughout history the ancient ones traveled,
    wandering the continents and sailing the oceans
    to discover rich lands with nurturing waters.
    Beating inside you are the steps that were taken,
    the obstacles conquered as they settled and roamed.
    In feelings whispering from deep in your heart,
    there comes a longing for a place to call home.
Putting down roots and planning for the future,
    each family then added their mutual efforts
    to establish a setting where all could flourish.

Your home is a garden in which you may grow,
    a deep well of strength giving courage to dare
    and a place of safe refuge where you are renewed.
    You can choose to relax in ways which are pleasing,
    joining with friends to converse and play music,
    preparing fine meals and competing in games
    or reading by the fire while listening to rainfall.
The house of your dreams will always be with you
    like a memory lingering from long in the past
    where you may retreat for your solace and rest.

Home

Following your vision wherever it leads,
    you quest for the comfort of a quiet haven
    as a base of confidence to reach for your goals.
    Do you prefer a beach house or city abode,
    a rambling farmhouse or mountain retreat,
    or perhaps a cottage or elegant estate?
    Where might you feel welcome and wish to share?
The special ambiance of the house you choose
    expresses the colors, textures and designs
    which serve as reflections of your taste and style.

When embarking to find your spiritual home,
    you begin a journey with receding horizons,
    pursuing the promise of paradise found,
    a domain of fulfillment with boundless love.
    As you open new vistas which draw you inside
    and quiet the turmoil of thoughts in your mind,
    you may find contentment wherever you are.
When life is complete, you will move off this sphere,
    borne gently away by an ethereal breeze
    to your ultimate peace in a heavenly home.

Sex

S ilhouetted by the pearlescent moonlight,
      your loved one awaits on the silvery shore,
      where sparkling sand is soft and inviting,
      and you reach out to touch your dream made real.
      The moments linger in long, warm embraces,
      stirring deep feelings concealed in your heart,
      willing to share of your innermost essence.
Yearning to release in total abandon,
      you merge like the river when joining the sea
      and surrender your will to the depths of desire.

Enchantment awaits in the dark of the night
      as steamy mists rise from pools under starlight;
      warm, velvet water caresses and holds you,
      as you float in the heavenly thrill of love's touch.
      Swept up in excitement you cannot deny,
      entering the realms where time is suspended,
      your thoughts drift away as the world disappears.
Caught by the strength of your deep adoration,
      as a willing captive who seeks no reprieve,
      your resistance dissolves in the charm of allure.

Sex

Time passes slowly when you must be parted,
      though memories bring comfort in hours alone,
      until once again you are with your beloved
      and can savor the feelings which both of you share.
      Life's quiet byways are filled with new meaning,
      attraction enraptures and emotions unfurl
      as the aura of romance swirls all around you.
Senses are heightened with each passing moment,
      the spell is enhanced by your love's tender kiss
      approaching the rapture of mystical union.

In loving caress like the foam on the shore,
      waves of sensation cascade between you
      with great tides of longing flooding your hearts.
      Pulses are quickened and breathing grows deeper,
      lifting you upward toward ecstasy's crown.
      Holding an instant at the height of your passion,
      you fall so gently into the fullness of love.
Emersed in a boundless feeling of oneness,
      the grand blending of spirits will open your soul
      to experience the moment when two are made whole.

Play

Reflecting the golden lightness of being
  through the art of pretending and make-believe,
  children lay spellbound in fields by the hour,
  watching wisps of clouds in which angels float by.
  They tiptoe through flowers and dance with fairies,
  turning in circles until so dizzy they fall,
  rolling over and over to laugh 'til they cry.
Adults walk too briskly and rarely take pause
  to peer in the darkness of hollowed out trees
  and discover the friends in which children believe.

The long summer days of childhood remembered,
  splashing and frolicking in the heat of the sun,
  napping on a log with a stream bubbling by,
  watching the sunlight dancing and sparkling,
  living each moment as though little else mattered.
  You may feel within a strong need to rekindle
  the visions you held when fantasy reigned.
Days go by quickly, the years vanish from view;
  worries and fears may cloud your perspective,
  and joys you once felt may have proven elusive.

Excitement and movement lift up your spirits,
      releasing the power within your emotions,
      so you can reclaim your passion and zeal.
      You might like the thrill of taking new risks,
      climbing steep cliffs or shooting the rapids,
      or you may find delight in collecting treasures,
      discovering rare coins, antiques or fine glass.
A mood of adventure can fill you with awe,
      providing a feeling of lightness and ease
      when the child within awakens from slumber.

There are worlds of pleasure to suit your taste
      where talents are tested and abilities shown:
      exploring the jungle or a mountain path,
      sowing a garden or refining a craft,
      reading a novel or rowing a boat,
      flying a kite or galloping on horseback,
      listening to music or playing a sport.
The price of admission is all of your cares,
      for the rules of the game are just to let go
      and learn to live life with a sense of abandon.

Work

$\mathcal{T}$ he gray squirrel collects nuts for the winter,
　　　scurrying up and down trees, hiding her cache.
　　　The beaver is tireless, constructing with twigs,
　　　creating a pond for a home and safe haven.
　　　People build structures wherever they settle
　　　for places to gather and wares to be sold
　　　in the ancient exchange of value for value.
Your work may be chosen from many careers,
　　　remaining near home or traveling afar,
　　　engaged in the mundane or creation of art.

Imagination can stir your excitement,
　　　and visions may form in response to desires,
　　　of ways you would like to provide a service
　　　and earn your living by means which inspire.
　　　Opportunities are waiting in the future
　　　with the chance to develop skills you will need
　　　to turn boring days into meaningful hours.
As choices arise, you may feel the intrigue
　　　of a question which too few would dare to ask:
　　　"If I were wealthy, what work would I do?"

When time moves so quickly there's none left for you,
    dreams drift away with each minute jammed full.
    You begin to feel numb as your spark becomes dim,
    and ideals soon fade as they lose their importance.
    If you think that you should always be active,
    not taking the time to unwind and relax,
    you will not give your most or perform at your best.
By reviewing schedules and plans for your days,
    weighing priorities that you might want to change,
    you can reach your goals with balance maintained.

Many pursuits are worthwhile and rewarding,
    and the work you select is a single measure,
    but only a part of your growth and fulfillment.
    Hobbies, travel and the time spent with friends
    offer changes of pace that give spice to your life,
    lifting the weight of the pressures you feel,
    increasing your sense of well being and pleasure.
Find your rewards in communion with people,
    and know that your tasks are true gifts to the world,
    with kindness and insight as the tools of your trade.

Travel

Traveling expands and widens horizons,
 providing novel and refreshing perspectives
 which help to fulfill your taste for excitement.
 Building the framework for your discernment,
 all you observe will add depth and substance
 as you learn from people in far away places
 and draw understanding from various viewpoints.
As ernest explorers, you seek the exotic,
 which seems so foreign from all you have known,
 and return with treasures of insights you've gained.

Cities and landscapes are stored as memories
 of sweeping panoramas and colorful scenes
 that surrounded you with vivid impressions:
 breathtaking vistas of mountains and seashores,
 hilltowns rising above rolling vineyards,
 historic museums holding grand collections
 and pastoral scenery as heart of the land.
Enthralled by wonders appearing around you,
 your soul is enriched by timely encounters,
 absorbing lifetimes in heartfelt connections.

Travel

The unknown calls you from around the corner,
    where soft mists follow a stream through the valley,
    leading to a village where children are playing.
    You are the stranger who walks among them,
    perhaps to be greeted as though long expected
    and find yourself sharing an intimate supper
    before moving on, throwing fate to the wind.
Adventure grows when firm plans are forgotten,
    and events come together like pieces of puzzles,
    forming the pictures where mystery prevails.

The outer world is a playground for senses,
    but the venture within is filled with intrigue.
    The inner realms have no end or beginning,
    for awareness may travel as free as the breeze
    and visit dimensions unguarded by time.
    Exploring the domains beyond mind or thought,
    you reach the heavens and touch the Divine.
Angels will show you the spheres of existence
    with luminous cities of crystalline splendor,
    where love grows and glistens in Gardens of Light.

Learning

Legends nourish your heart and excite the mind
    with mysteries, dramas and stories of valor.
    In endless battles with victories and defeats,
    the villains and heroes marched into history.
    Conquerors and artists, reformers and priests
    strolled through the streets of their ancient cities,
    leaving their chronicles for others to teach.
Knowledge gathered from all of the centuries
    may offer lessons which serve you today
    to help avoid error and build upon brilliance.

Children are born into customs and cultures,
    like strangers who arrive from another land
    trying to determine their way in this world.
    Absorbing language and rules of acceptance,
    they learn from mentors who speak from experience
    and find that each person has stories to tell,
    while daily struggles may hide gems of wisdom.
Like a writer's journal with empty pages,
    young minds are open to imprint new ideas,
    yet deep understanding is more than just words.

True education emerges through living,
> though much can be gained from courses of study.
> Philosophy finds meaning in thought and reason,
> science is founded on facts and strict logic,
> psychology tries to explain human nature,
> art speaks the language of feelings and beauty,
> yet the search for truth does not end in a class.
You may learn that real insight cannot be taught,
> for keys must be forged to unlock inner vision
> to see your direction and reason for being.

Your hunger for knowledge and information
> may lead to libraries of crowded confusion;
> but if courage takes you on roads less traveled,
> you may attain what wisemen continue to seek.
> You need not have riches or personal power
> to achieve the wealth of spiritual teachings,
> for with earnest intent your goal will be reached.
Within your heart is a window to heaven,
> where perception is clear and all can be seen,
> revealing the essence of Ultimate Truth.

Laughter

Laughter will refresh and lift up your spirit,
  dissolving dark shadows in glowing brightness,
  adding times of delight to enliven the day.
  Spontaneous people with a sense of freedom
  enhance all they do with their cheerful demeanor
  and are rarely submerged in the depths of drama,
  for they quickly shift to a lightness of being.
Humor hides between joy and irreverence,
  a slight discomfort on this side of offense
  where a fine line divides your laughter from tears.

Life is a sequence of actors and stages,
  yet when caught in illusion, it all seems so real.
  With brow deeply furrowed, you can be convincing
  and forget you are acting when lost in the play.
  What if each scene were viewed as a comedy?
  The woeful extremes might even be funny,
  like a raft full of tricksters being dumped in a stream.
Jesters perform with parody and satire;
  clowns leap in the air, then tumble and fall;
  though the masks are sad, their wild antics amuse.

Laughter

Witness children as they frolic together,
      expressing their spirited nature and style,
      showing elation which bubbles up freely;
      smitten with giggles, they turn topsy-turvey.
      Innocent of cares, untroubled by worries,
      the young are tickled by the silliest stories
      and fall into laughter for no reason at all.
If a childlike excitement were to fill you
      and each day were viewed as a game to be played,
      you might greet the morning with wondrous delight.

What if your smile were the key to life's fortunes,
      bringing you friendship and unforeseen pleasures?
      Perhaps an outlook which feels much less somber
      could be just the ticket for shedding your burdens.
      You may find new ways to lean into laughter,
      making fun of yourself as you toss pride away,
      entering enjoyment with sadness departing.
To expand your full sense of humor and joy,
      you may release the weight of more serious views,
      and the happiness longed for will soon overflow.

Abudance

As seeds regenerate like stars being born,
the universe is breathing life in abundance.
Flowering trees absorb the warm sunlight,
sending forth baskets of fruit from the orchard.
Waves of grain sparkle like gold in the fields,
and the oceans share in their plentiful harvest,
displaying the earth's great fertility and fullness.
The inheritance of man is all around,
and gifts of benevolence flow like spring showers
to hearts that have opened to fully receive.

Creation emerges as the large and small;
tiny worlds are held in the charge of atoms,
and massive galaxies expand into forever.
Some people worry about futures imagined
when they might be lost, alone and untended.
Increasing awareness of balance and order
will reveal each one's part in a much larger plan.
The fear of lack that creates a foreboding
is borne from the dread of famine and warfare;
though plenty abounds, it may seem to elude you.

Abundance

Prosperity is held in your point of view,
    and contentment is found in everyday pleasures,
    not held in the luxuries of which you soon tire.
    Simple delights are a home filled with caring,
    the warmth of a fire when winter winds blow,
    tasting fresh bread being served from the oven,
    and the colors of sunrise which start each day new.
True wealth is the richness you feel deep inside;
    with no urge to possess, your coffers are full,
    for when tithing with love, it returns many fold.

The more you are emptied, the more you are filled;
    your cup runs over with sweet nectar revealed.
    The heavens pour rain on earth far below,
    sending rivers and streams cascading downhill,
    rushing through forests and over great falls,
    echoing in canyons, streaming across prairies,
    nourishing life as it winds toward the sea.
As a wellspring from the source of your being,
    the gifts that you give are your fortunes received;
    when sharing your all, there is little you need.

Food & Drink

Y ou are caretaker of your holy body,
a sacred vessel for the Spirit on earth.
You gather sustenance from nature's bounty,
rich fibre and textures of greens and legumes,
the burst of sweetness in freshly picked fruits,
all borne through the alchemy of mother earth
and sending forth the energy of father sun.
Consciousness glows at the heart of your being,
with embers fanned by the breath of life,
expanded and heightened in radiance and love.

A banquet for royalty sits before you,
as food for thought to entice your mind:
breaking the bread of shared opinions,
biting into a spicy exchange of viewpoints,
cutting to the center of delicious theories,
dipping in the richness of a heated debate
and savoring the taste of sweet ambrosia.
You are the arbiter of all decisions,
the foods you eat and which feelings to hold,
your recipes for health of both body and soul.

Food & Drink

In the midst of abundance, craving is found;
        a drought of compassion has spread deprivation
        as sorrow and sadness have filled empty hearts.
        There is a longing to sip nature's essence
        and taste the quintessence of heavenly truth,
        but illusion obscures like layers of icing
        which may be dissolved in elixirs of light.
For those who desire to fulfill their life's quest,
        seeds of hope must be planted in soils of faith
        and cared for as a gardener who watches over.

Raw foods give you strength and water will cleanse you,
        but there are other needs which food cannot fill.
        The thirst of your spirit is quenched with wisdom,
        and your soul's deep hunger is met only with love.
        You may open the door to a limitless storehouse
        where the Kingdom's harvest is offered to you,
        and the wealth is yours, for the Host is most gracious.
As a being of light fed by Creation,
        your body is nurtured and your soul is sustained
        by the nectar of life received through God's Love.

Environment

A s the living library of creation,
earth's nursery greets the changes of season,
adorning the meadows with garlands of flowers,
providing homes for a multitude of creatures.
Through splendid designs of interdependence,
without true boundaries and no clear divisions,
life abounds in complex systems of balance.
Nature's grandeur of woven relationships
between rivers and land, oceans and sky
generates the atmosphere for all existence.

Various forms emerged over eons of time
as a wondrous experiment of living art,
displaying the beauty of infinite vision.
Inhabiting continents, swimming in oceans
and soaring to heights far above the clouds,
all beings have their own missions to fill
and each part has importance within nature's plan.
Plants and trees cover the land with great flourish,
providing shelter and giving nourishment
while serving as theaters of interaction.

Environment

Bear cubs are huddled in caves through the winter,
    arising in spring to catch fish in the streams
    and to climb up branches in search of honey.
    The lioness stretches and leaves her lair,
    followed by kittens, romping and wrestling.
    They learn from elders the art of survival
    and are guided by instincts to live in the wild.
Animals have their own ways of relating,
    from the lone traveler to group migrations
    which move in concert as if sharing one mind.

Your home environment strongly affects you,
    surrounded by beauty or careless disorder;
    when filled with your favorite designs and colors,
    it may brighten your feelings and state of mind.
    Borne of the earth and formed from its essence,
    mankind was entrusted with this fragile system,
    and the future of life is held in the balance.
You were given dominion over nature,
    to cherish the planet with love and safekeeping,
    as you grow like the mystical rose in life's garden.

Beauty

B eauty is a night bird perched among the leaves,
       singing sweet lullabies to stars unseen.
       Loveliness is the warmth of a mother's smile,
       children out dancing in the soft summer rain,
       butterflies resting on colorful flowers,
       sunbeams sparkling across glassy ponds,
       and wisps of willows that sway in the breeze.
Elegance is nature unwinding seasons
       in an ardent display of constant rebirth,
       animating the land with lush flora and fauna.

You define the ideal in limited ways,
       with the bloom of youth far more favored than age.
       Yet, majesty can be seen in wrinkled faces
       and grand, ancient canyons carved in the land,
       or in towering redwoods streaming emerald light,
       in showers of meteors streaking the heavens,
       and in northern lights which emblazon the sky.
Emotions respond when senses are flooded
       with perceptions that stir the core of your being
       and help to awaken your timeless awareness.

Beauty

Artists inhale all the grandeur around them
　　　and breathe out a personal view of existence:
　　　through paintings of seascapes with crashing waves,
　　　in sculptures of marble embodied with form,
　　　with symphonic melodies which thrill the heart,
　　　through inspiring poems received from the Muse,
　　　and in songs that arise out of exquisite verse.
In the passion of creative endeavors
　　　are emotions the artist brings into being,
　　　radiating an essence expressed by the soul.

Beauty can never be explained or measured,
　　　since all aspects of life are sacred in nature,
　　　mixed from a palette of dazzling colors
　　　and painted in subtle patterns of harmony.
　　　The universe unfolds like flowers blooming
　　　with petals opening into cosmic design,
　　　reflecting the brilliance of the Divinity.
You embody the splendor of the Master
　　　as a fountain flowing in shimmering perfection,
　　　a jewel that shines in the crown of creation.

Music

The Word came forth as the sound of formation,
    the breath of existence and mystical source,
    and humans emerged as echoes of Spirit
    reaching through time to inhabit the earth.
    Light and sound unify in waves of connection,
    space and time blending as texture and form
    as the concert of life plays a prelude of love.
There are heavenly notes intoned by the spheres,
    of beautiful melodies in and around you
    with celestial harmonics weaving their spell.

The music of nature, a soft serenade,
    will help to release the stress you have held.
    Attuning yourself to the sounds of the forest,
    whispers of water are heard from a streambed,
    worries take flight on the wind through the trees,
    peace fills the love songs two mourning doves sing,
    and senses are cleansed by rain falling on leaves.
The universe lives in constant vibration,
    sustaining awareness in physical form
    and dancing to rhythms your mind has not heard.

Music

The power of music pierces your being,
 inviting your smiles and releasing your tears,
 and songs from the past may pull you through time
 to return with memories refreshed and renewed.
 When offering yourself as an instrument,
 you will feel a sense of harmony building
 with ethereal magic welling up from inside.
Your part is performed through your feelings and words;
 you are the music and master composer,
 sharing the depth of your own inspiration.

In a boundless symphony's infinite themes,
 you may hear the refrain of a clarion call
 in the hypnotic beating of primitive drums,
 or the refined perfection of an orchestra's strings.
 Your heart responds to the richness and depth
 with extremes of emotion often aroused,
 from urges of passion to reverence and awe.
The true secrets of sound that live in your heart
 will reveal the mystery of music within,
 and your voice will be joined in a chorus of love.

Time

The sun peaks over a crimson horizon,
    lifting the curtain of night from the land.
    You stir and awaken from out of your slumber
    with consciousness held in a timeless realm,
    a gap between thoughts where clarity reigns
    where peace can be found in a view of forever
    and the truth is known about time without end.
When you move your focus out of the present
    and are caught in past sorrows or future desires,
    you may miss the richness surrounding you now.

Awareness dissolves in thoughts of tomorrow
    and disappears quickly in yesterday's dream.
    The ancients lived on the outskirts of time
    where history was learned from stories and songs.
    Their minds were not haunted by musty old pictures,
    nor always consumed in thoughts of the future;
    they focused their plans on the needs of the day.
When you become trapped inside of past worries,
    overwhelmed by concerns with vision clouded,
    you may pause in the moment to see your way clear.

Time

When setting the schedules which structure your days,
    you may feel the weight of unending demands.
    It is hard to imagine a life not controlled
    by constant reminders of time passing by
    with a code of numbers you learned to heed,
    of when you must go and when to return
    and how fast you must hurry not to be late.
If days were not broken into minutes and hours
    and the sun's position were your only guide,
    you might feel a wholeness outside of time's spell.

With the worthy goal of shedding your limits,
    you may wish to elude time's invisible hold
    and find a new freedom beyond its restrictions.
    Emerging as spirit in a physical form,
    like a wave lifting out of the ocean of being
    which flows up the beach and returns to the depths,
    you rise in the flesh, then rejoin the infinite.
Time has no power beyond its illusion,
    and you can escape from the pull of the trance
    to live in the timeless experience of now.

Sin

A seasoned sailor follows charts for the voyage,
measuring distances and gauging the wind.
Slight deviations of the rudder or compass
will divert a ship from the planned destination.
Like sailing off course, sin is missing the port,
losing direction from the source of all truth,
while error and trespass bring pain in their wake.
Each action sets chains of events in motion,
reactions returning through circles of time,
with cause and effect as your mirrors for learning.

Those without purpose are lost in a fog bank,
unable to find their way in the world.
With vision diffused, confusion is swirling;
moving in blindness, the markers are hidden,
and signs are not seen by the wayward to follow.
In desperation, they may turn to survival,
with ways and means being of little concern.
Waves of emotion may knock you off balance,
throwing you into the cold churning sea
to sink like a stone in the depths of despair.

Sin

When you turn away from a lighthouse beacon
      and are lost and adrift in the blackness of night,
      a time may come when all hope is abandoned
      and you pray to heaven that you might be saved.
      If you are truly willing to alter your course,
      to surrender the helm and bring about faith,
      you will catch the first glimmer of dawn as it breaks.
The dreadful darkness is eased with the sighting
      of light which illumines the passage ahead
      as you sail homeward bound upon winds of change.

You are born in this world to embrace your life
      as a treasure received from the One Creator.
      Though many believe you should live in fear
      of being condemned to eternal damnation,
      it will serve you far better to open your heart
      and wash away guilt with the power of love,
      knowing God has forgiven before you would ask.
Keep sight on the future and do not look back,
      for the Lord of All is now calling you forth
      with lightness of spirit to break free from the past.

Prayer

Parents say prayers for the blessing of children,
bringing their love and heartfelt thanksgiving,
knowing that God is aware of their needs.
Circles of prayer are formed by the faithful
to assist those with burdens too heavy to bear,
asking for insight when doubts have arisen,
believing in earnest their requests will be heard.
Angels would like to provide all your wishes,
yet they see to the core of your soul's true desire
and help show the way to your life's higher plan.

Placing your faith in a loving Creator
and striving to perceive where meaning is hidden,
you will learn from events which seem to confound.
When moved by your prayers into calm contentment,
you will find a stillness where fears fade from view,
and the strength you require is discovered within
as your heart overflows in the peace of God's Love.
Heavenly messengers bring you their blessings
of assurance and courage to move through your pain
and discover the source of your own salvation.

Prayer

You may hold onto fears that block acceptance
     and maintain beliefs which no longer serve you;
     yet, when asking for guidance from a higher power,
     your limiting thoughts will be quickly dissolved.
     Expressing your thanks for all you've been given
     and sensing the bliss of your future fulfillment,
     you will find you are open to truly receive.
When harboring doubts and caught in confusion,
     you may sense the temptation to feel undeserving,
     but worthiness is not the key to prayers answered.

The power of prayer is not found in pleading,
     but comes to those who feel love in their hearts
     and are willing to see what is best for their growth.
     Each of your prayers will set forces in motion,
     though solutions hoped for may not come to pass,
     and the purpose for problems may be confusing,
     but with time the true reasons are often revealed.
Since the world around you is always changing,
     tomorrow's events can never be known,
     thus the prayer for all seasons is "Thy will be done."

Religion

From time immemorial humans have tried
 to peer beyond the mundane and into heaven.
 Observing the wonder of nature displayed,
 they bowed with reverence to concepts of God.
 Down through the ages the world has been given
 great masters and saints, the prophets and sages, *babies)*
 who offered their wisdom to all who would hear.
Religion was born when people were gathered,
 agreeing to share their clues to the mystery,
 revealing their knowledge and insights on truth.

Places of worship stir adoration
 in hallowed assemblies with lofty intent,
 where each one may find a renewed dedication
 to serve with love and the spirit of fellowship.
 Rituals consecrate the milestones of life,
 from the greeting of newborns to solemn farewells,
 honoring the passages and hallmarks of time.
Religions give seekers of similar views
 a sense of support in the midst of their doubts,
 and beliefs are enhanced as meaning is found.

Having faith and trust in the Supreme Being
    confers a peace which exceeds understanding,
    with courage to prevail through constant changes.
    The pleasure of friends with common ideals
    may be enjoyed in a spiritual family,
    all linked by the vision of loving devotion
    and sharing their dreams of heaven and earth.
Religions aspire to fulfill a mission
    of providing teachings and inspiration
    and giving their guidance for the journey ahead.

The Source of Creation transcends all thinking;
    no name or description can be sufficient,
    for the nature of God is beyond definition.
    Those who experience the awesome grandeur
    may attempt to explain their feelings of bliss;
    though words can never express the rapture,
    their selfless compassion brings grace to the world.
Those who enter the higher realms of being
    see through the illusion and into the light
    and reflect the magnificent glory of love.

Courage

ANIMO-VALOR

𝒯 ales of great courage are woven in stories
and read to young children while falling asleep
to dream of grand heroes with noble ideals,
inspiring the wish to be fearless and daring.
People who carry the wounded from battle
or risk all they have to assist those in need
join with the brave who are striving for peace.
When faced with danger or threatened by peril,
valor is often performed without question,
demanding quick action with no thought of safety.

Decisions needed may require fresh resolve,
for resistance becomes an obstinate rival.
Attachments and friendships tend to restrain,
even when knowing a change must be made.
Though the contest at hand may not be apparent,
an heroic image can serve in your quandary,
bolstering your valiance to live each day boldly.
The road ahead presents unforeseen challenge;
yet following guidance your course will be steady,
and with strength of purpose, your steps will be sure.

Courage may decree control and forbearance
  to await the right moment for you to respond,
  and a trial of patience may test your endurance,
  getting lost in the details of what must be done.
  If you risk your resources, time and effort
  on ventures inspired by your heartfelt beliefs,
  you place more than a wager when betting on faith.
Preparing yourself for the unexpected,
  you will greet the unknown with growing excitement
  and leap the dark chasms without hesitation.

In choosing to live a life filled with meaning,
  you draw from within for strength you may need
  to help a young child learn to rise above fear
  or launch a movement to bring about justice,
  search for a cure on the frontiers of research,
  fight for the freedom of a people enslaved,
  or create a poem which touches one heart.
Allow yourself to receive Spirit's Power,
  feel confidence soar as you brave life's demands,
  and lift your sights to surmount the impossible.

Miracles

E ach aspect of life from molecules to stars,
    water to fire and the very air that you breathe,
    can be explained up to a point of departure
    where the unknown is shrouded in mystery.
    An egg and sperm will unite and multiply,
    becoming the cells of heart, lungs and nerves,
    forming a complex and conscious new being.
Nature creates from primary elements,
    swirling together through infinite networks,
    in which the awareness of God is imbued.

Miraculous healings defy description;
    amazing events and strange phenomena
    have been recorded throughout the ages.
    Science has sought to shine light on enigmas,
    unraveling the threads of ancient mythology,
    stretching the boundaries of current knowledge
    and calming the fears which have haunted mankind.
Miracles reveal a world of great wonder,
    for they bear the imprint of Spirit at work
    transcending the limits of logical thought.

Miracles

Expanding intentions and expectations,
     you begin to demolish walls of restriction
     and soon find yourself in the midst of a riddle.
     Looking through shallow facades of appearance,
     you see with the vision which consciousness brings,
     your desires are answered in mysterious ways,
     receiving the wealth and reward of your dreams.
From the grand sea of all possibility,
     spontaneous cures and great turns of fortune
     will emerge and become the natural order.

You have been searching for wisdom and knowledge
     with a passion to know your reason for being,
     hoping the wise would provide you with answers
     and asking for guidance when plans went awry.
     You have had encounters which seem preordained,
     auspicious meetings surpassing coincidence
     with synchronous timing you could not explain.
You are living within a vortex of change
     where laws of reality are turned inside out
     with glorious miracles surrounding you now.

Meditation

Gray eventide rolls gently over the shore
    as bright strokes of rose cast graceful designs
    on iridescent shades of a sunset aglow.
    Settling into comfort and feeling at ease,
    relaxing all tension and slowing your breathing,
    and focusing awareness between your eyebrows,
    you will sense the warmth of your own inner light.
Meditation creates an aura of peace,
    when concerns are surrendered and love is embraced,
    and your heart is revealed as a state of pure being.

Emotions may arise and gain their control,
    spinning thought circles with words repeating,
    anchoring your spirit in restless foreboding.
    Thinking is calmed if you shift your attention:
    imagine your mind drifting down to your naval,
    like watching a pebble dropping into a pool,
    coming to rest on the smooth, sandy bottom.
Your thoughts will float upward like bubbles toward air
    to burst on the surface and just disappear;
    then bring your focus back to your center.

Deep meditation clarifies your viewpoint
  as issues and upsets retreat in the distance,
  and your worries and fears start fading away.
  Learning to flow with continuous change
  and becoming aware of resistance and judgments,
  you empty your mind to live in the moment
  and feel to the core of your own inner truth.
Exploring beyond your physical being,
  you may open the curtains to mystical worlds
  and observe the mansions of celestial realms.

Your inner sight may view patterns and colors,
  spinning mandalas which pulsate with brilliance.
  You might see a lake without wind or ripple,
  reflecting the beauty of bright autumn leaves
  as you enter the hush of serene contentment.
  And from the silence a presence may beckon,
  awakening your soul to a divine romance.
Your consciousness is a mirror of heaven,
  which absorbs and reflects great love and wisdom
  as treasures from God to behold and to share.

Good & Evil

Grand summits offer sharp rocks and steep ridges
 as dangerous climbs for those without skill,
 yet the view from the peak will leave you in awe.
The ocean has riptides and deadly currents
 which may carry swimmers away from the shore,
 while divers below will exalt the sea's beauty.
 Are the heights or deep water a blessing or curse?
Appearances shift depending on outlook:
 the way you perceive is your personal view,
 which is filtered through lenses of love or fear.

Events in your life may lead you to ponder:
 do guidelines exist to know right from wrong,
 and can truth be found in religion or law?
 If a war can be just, is all killing sinful?
 Are generous gifts always righteous or kind?
 There are no easy answers to draw a clear line,
 for the rosebud blossoms, yet falls to the ground.
If you split and label the wholeness of life,
 though attempting to fathom its meaning,
 you may be lost in concepts of absolute truth.

Good & Evil

When your actions come from loving intention,
    but someone is hurt and finds you at fault,
    release the guilt which can weigh on your soul,
    for life brings veiled lessons for the learning of all.
    Do not be imprisoned by worry or dread,
    hiding yourself from a vengeance imagined,
    for God's only offering is wisdom and love.
The challenges you face may seem harsh or cruel,
    yet within your life are patterns repeating,
    created by the choices you made or ignored.

If you see a world in which evil abounds
    and Satan is blamed for upsets and sorrows,
    you are giving control to an idea grown weary
    with solutions untapped and answers untold.
    When you ask why you feel such anguish and pain,
    you may find your turmoil is often self-made,
    for free will permits you to rise up or to fall.
Releasing judgement, you will know the heart's way,
    with a Spirit of Holiness living within you
    to guide all your steps through the baptism of love.

Pain & Suffering

The wheel of life spins the clay of creation;
    from the potter's strong hands your being is formed,
    swept deep and shaped high as a powerful vessel.
    Tempered and strengthened in the heat of the kiln,
    emblazoned by fire to set your true colors,
    you hold silent tears of your pain and desire
    and look to the heavens for answers to come.
Time leaves its traces, your surface is weathered;
    the wind blows through you in echoes of mourning
    for memories held secret and love left unspoken.

Dreams may be scattered like leaves in the autumn
    to appear that misfortune unfairly prevails,
    and you wonder aloud what meaning is hidden
    as the seasons move on into winter's cold chill.
    The plan for your life is not one to suffer,
    though pain and strife are so often involved,
    and the truth that you seek may lay your soul bare.
When you are lost in a state of confusion,
    retrace the steps that you recently made,
    for with your free choice you may wander astray.

Pain & Suffering

When caught in despair, you may turn from guidance,
    closing your eyes to the signs all around you,
    with ears that are deaf to truth being spoken
    and a heart unwilling to share what it knows.
    If you have been clinging to anguish and torment,
    uncover the ways your mind would control,
    resolve to release and surrender your hold.
When you are alone and feeling abandoned,
    you may think that your love will never return;
    but remember with time even broken hearts mend.

The truth of life is everything changes;
    there are no exceptions to this simple rule.
    Take comfort in knowing pain finally ceases;
    take warning if you would resist what is new.
    Things of value may soon lose their meaning,
    possessions you claim will someday be gone,
    and events of the future can seldom be seen.
Rejoice at your pleasure and bow to your pain,
    for moments are fleeting in both joy and sorrow,
    and what stands before you shall never be again.

Spiritual Growth

Growing like the wild pear grasping at a cliff,
　　you cling to the known, afraid to let go
　　and peer through a fog of shadowy memories,
　　watching people and places retreat in the mist.
　　Awakening slowly, the cliff fades from view;
　　a pathway of mystery appears before you,
　　and with your first steps, the long journey begins.
Ready to feel your connection with Spirit,
　　you develop a wider perspective of life
　　and uncover the truth which you had not perceived.

At first you are wary, but soon gain courage,
　　crossing over bridges which span dimensions.
　　You may look back, yet your heart hears a calling
　　to discover the realms where visions are born.
　　When your fears and desires release their control,
　　mind and emotions become peaceful and calm,
　　and questions no longer seem to need answers.
Transcending beliefs once holding you captive,
　　old patterns and habits are left in the past
　　as you grow into faith and awareness expands.

Spiritual Growth

Whether you live in a natural setting
     or move through a city's busy commotion,
     you cannot abandon the path of your growth,
     for the place where you learn is right where you are.
     The guidance received from your intuition
     can lead you on to your purpose for living
     and open your heart to know Divine Will.
Flashes of insight will provide directions
     when you learn to take heed of that soft inner voice
     and discern what you hear as a pillar of truth.

In your spiritual quest to find fulfillment,
     you will begin to focus and balance your mind
     while expanding your sight to a grand overview.
     In stories of travels through mystical domains,
     those searching for wisdom met with great challenge
     as they claimed rare secrets and sacred powers,
     then emerged to teach from their wholeness of being.
Wayshowers of peace bring love and compassion,
     and in their reflection your Self may be seen,
     so you may rejoice in the light of your knowing.

Forgiveness

When a gale wind blows, the palm trees arch over,
standing upright after the storm passes by.
Living through the turmoil and tempest of life,
feeling the anguish from anger or scorn,
you, too, may be bent by the weight of sadness.
If you can excuse and dismiss what has happened,
a new day will dawn to stand tall once more.
Memories are stories in which you have lived,
and some are recalled with upset and blame,
yet forgiveness is needed for you to move on.

Wheels of illusion spiral ever upward,
presenting lessons of higher perspectives
in fateful events which emerge like a dream.
To justify hatred and violent actions,
humans sustained the concept of vengeance
with an eye for an eye, and a tooth for a tooth,
the law of the past in which all were consumed.
The goal has been changed to one of forgiveness,
suspending your ire and leaving resentment,
so hearts can be healed in the salve of your love.

Forgiveness

Forgiving does not declare an approval;
    you need not condone the issues at hand.
    By removing yourself, your emotions diffuse,
    avoiding the impulse to seek swift reprisal.
    When bearing no malice and making amends,
    you dissolve the thoughts that lead to reaction
    and stem the flow of the course toward revenge.
Caught in the midst of frustration and anger,
    you may live with pain and the weight of depression
    until loosening the chains of tangled attachments.

There are none without need to forswear their guilt,
    for freedom is measured in terms of your mercy
    toward those who trespass and shame that you bear.
    Unleash the love from your sacred center,
    so your heart can expand with full compassion,
    and do not forget to include your own being,
    as you grant forgiveness and embrace life again.
Loving yourself and those who surround you
    requires acceptance and sincere understanding,
    and by truly forgiving, your soul is set free.

Surrender

The battle cry calls the warriors to action;
    for personal reasons, each one fights to win.
    The thought of surrender is never considered
    until all appears futile with nothing to gain.
    Problems and trauma may form your dissent,
    or passionate feelings can hinder clear vision
    and lock your mind in a cell of constriction.
When at a crossroads, be wise and take notice,
    determine which choices led you on detours,
    and expose the excuses you made to hold on.

This earthly sojourn can be very lonely
    when you feel empty and meaning has faded,
    detached from others and even the Creator.
    In truth you are joined with all of existence
    like sunlight streaming down through the foliage,
    casting designs as it sparkles and dances,
    apart yet connected to one source of light.
When yielding yourself to a greater power,
    you will witness a strength which is waiting within
    and learn that God's Will is your true heart's desire.

Surrender

Behind your tenacious attempts to control
    is the dread of losing the things you have gained;
    yet when this life passes, all you've gathered is gone.
    When worry is surrendered, time will expand,
    and your strong sense of urgency starts to recede.
    By living in faith that your efforts are guided,
    you will see that the dragons are only your fears.
Beyond the problems that seem to slow progress
    is a grander intent supporting your goals,
    which will lift you out of the deep cave of darkness.

Like ribbons unwrapping presents from angels,
    the tight grip of confinement loosens its hold
    and reveals the gifts that have long been awaited,
    which will fill your heart and enlighten your soul.
    In place of impatience, you float in contentment,
    with tensions released, your guard is let down,
    and you know your life is in Spirit's safekeeping.
The light of the heavens will shine in the night
    with moonlight revealing the pathway ahead,
    as you take your place in the footsteps of Masters.

Gratitude

Gratitude plays a heart song of reverence
    when you behold wonder in all you perceive
    and feel the assurance of love which endures.
    Like a flawless diamond refracting the light
    when the sun brightens its crystalline form,
    your illumined facets glisten with color,
    reflecting your spirit resplendent within.
Thankfulness invites your appreciation,
    with attitude shaping your view of the world
    and supporting awareness of blessings around you.

Arising to greet the birth of a new day,
    you welcome the gifts of life being offered:
    the soft morning breeze, warm water to bathe,
    your body responding with a graceful ease,
    flavorful foods which supply health and vigor,
    friends who accept you for just who you are,
    along with experience to quicken your growth.
With freedom to choose which direction to take,
    each day is a canvas on which you can paint
    benedictions to the Source of all creation.

Gratitude

Life's twists and sharp turns may impede your journey,
with your mind rebelling like an untamed stallion,
kicking the fence with the need to run free.
If you are hemmed in by rails of your making,
held firmly in place by your rigid control,
be hobbled no more by shackles that bind you:
throw off the harness and escape with your soul.
Celebrate your freedom in gratitude found,
setting in motion grand forces unseen,
the mystery and magic to manifest dreams.

Events are cloaked in perplexing disguises,
presenting you clues in which fate plays a hand;
with opportune moments to uncover meaning,
you catch subtle hints of the truth you might find.
Gratefulness unlocks the gates of receiving,
allowing for gifts to be brought unto you,
and the joy you express is your thankfulness shown.
Without judgement of success or misfortune,
you may live in faith that your trust is upheld,
with growing awareness of perfection unveiled.

Angels

With our love we quiet the night storm's tempest,
  ready to shield you from harm that might call.
  As the living countenance of Love Eternal,
  we come as translators of the Truth Divine.
  Standing our vigil with constant devotion,
  we give our comfort to set minds at ease
  and sustain the faith of all those in need.
With boundless joy we bestow our compassion,
  shining our light to illumine your way
  bringing good fortune on the pilgrimage home.

As radiant beings who need not slumber,
  we open the doors to spiritual realms,
  hovering at the mystical edge of time
  where sleep turns to dreams and souls learn to fly.
  Our charge is to awaken you from illusion
  and speak to your heart in the language of love
  with the guidance to follow your life's higher plan.
Know you are blessed with a guardian angel,
  a friend and companion traveling beside you,
  to aid in your search for answers and meaning.

Angels

Our wings may be glimpsed at the rim of vision
or viewed in the sunbeams which dance in the sky.
As messengers of God we come in service,
prepared to support you through all of your trials,
offering our counsel through whispers of caring.
With deep understanding, we impart our insight
and present the great treasure of infinite peace.
You are born to live this life in its fullness,
to embrace and honor all seen and unseen
and join with the angels of heaven on earth.

Showering you with unbounded awareness
that flows through us as a blessing from Spirit,
we are holy keepers of the watch for mankind,
surrounding you in our eternal protection.
Our voices lift up with inspired adoration,
singing the praise of our Lord and Creator,
author of miracles and grand inspiration.
As heavenly hosts exalting God's Glory,
we reveal that love is your reason for being
and proclaim the splendor of life everlasting.

Death

What is death? you ask when youth is on your brow.
What happens when people have passed away?
Do they still exist, and where have they gone?
They have shed the body and lifted the veil,
and traveled to realms where their spirit may dwell.
Received by their loved ones and angels of light,
they are blessed and anointed by heavenly hosts.
What is death? you may ask as you grow in age.
You will feel yourself rise from this earthly stage;
transcending illusion, soul and spirit are freed.

Upon the turning wheel of life and of death,
you are born to live and someday will die;
as sure as the sun rises, by nightfall it sets.
All that is living will evolve by its nature,
with eternity given to save each one's soul.
Dreams within dreams will reveal their meaning
when you are awakened from your silken repose.
Life is an offering to live with freedom,
creating and reaping in the ways you have sown,
and your measure of wealth is love you have shared.

Death

Those who would fear the final ebb of their tide
      may need to remember a promise of old:
      you are truly loved and are never alone.
      Be at peace as you think of your last day on earth,
      for in your surrender God's Grace will be shown,
      and walking in the valley of the shadow of death,
      you will know that the pathway is taking you home.
Though you may not recall these words as written,
      from your heart will arise a feeling of bliss,
      providing assurance at your time to depart.

There is an angel, your guardian spirit,
      who assists you now and will love you forever,
      a guide for your life, through death and thereafter,
      awaiting the moment to show you the way.
      You will feel Divine Presence enfolding your being
      and see golden light that shines through your soul,
      as a peace sublime lifts you up into heaven.
Though words are not spoken, you will understand;
      overflowing with love, awareness expands,
      and reborn as spirit, your grand journey begins.

The Window is located on South Ridge Trail, which leads to the nine thousand foot Tahquitz Peak, overlooking the town of Idyllwild in the San Bernardino National Forest in Southern California.

Verlaine Crawford is author of the book *Ending the Battle Within* in which she shares her insights on how to create a joyful and fulfilling life. She presents workshops around the world and is an inspirational speaker.